WHAT'S *LOVE* GOT TO DO WITH IT?

Strengthen your marriage,
and discover the many aspects of love.

LONNIE E. RILEY, D.Min. &
KIMBERLY T. RILEY, M.Div.

WHAT'S *LOVE* GOT TO DO WITH IT?

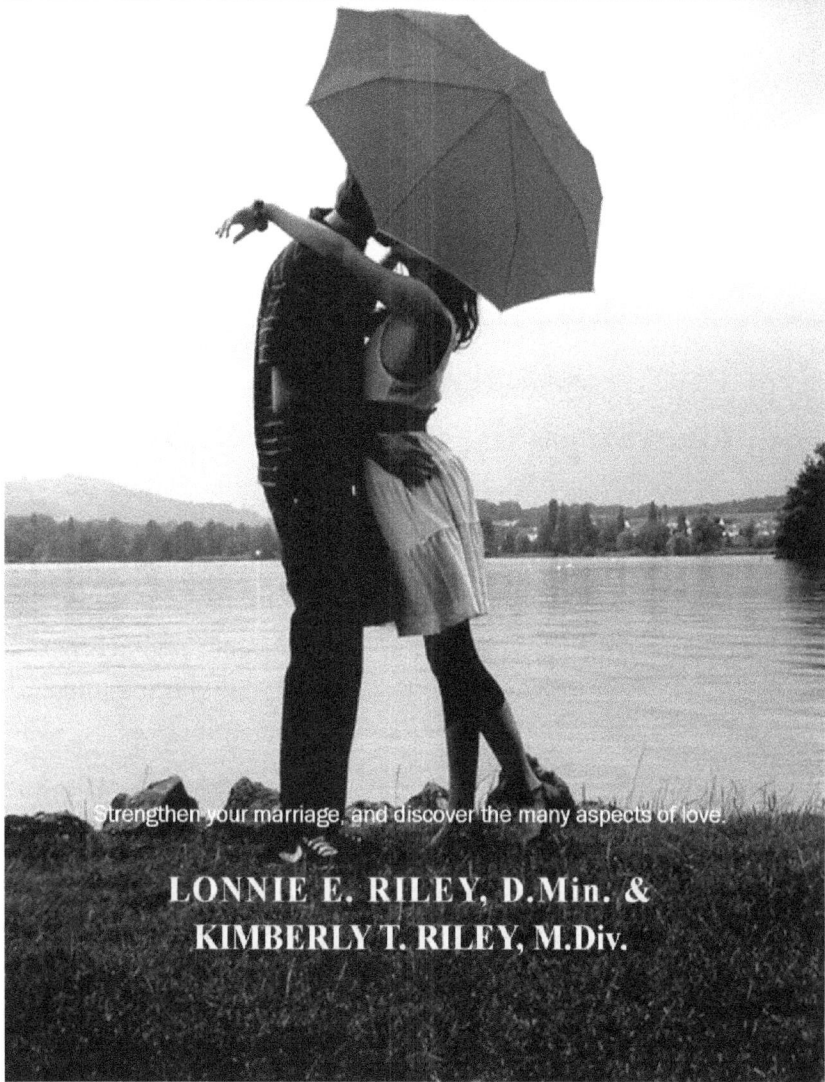

Strengthen your marriage, and discover the many aspects of love.

LONNIE E. RILEY, D.Min. &
KIMBERLY T. RILEY, M.Div.

What's Love Got To Do With It?
by Lonnie E. Riley, D.Min. and Kimberly T. Riley, M.Div.

ISBN: 978-0-9884455-2-9

Cover Design: Kimberly T. Riley

Published in 2013 by
Published by Freedom Place Publishing

A Division of Freedom Ministries International
Myrtle Beach, SC
www.fmintl.org

Library of Congress Control Number: 2013954475

Printed in the United States of America

CONTENTS

DEDICATION

We dedicate this book to our dear friends and co-workers at Freedom Ministries International, Jim and Joy Odom. They have served God, each other, and us faithfully over the years and exemplify the meaning of Christian LOVE.

Thank you for your constant prayers and support, and for always being our true friends.

"This is My commandment, that you love one another as I have loved you. Greater love has no one than this, than to lay down one's life for his friends."
John 15:12-13 (NKJV)

INTRODUCTION

"What's love got to do with it?" This is the title of a song that you may be familiar with. It says that love is just a "second hand emotion." However, love is much more than that, especially in the context of marriage.

You will look over the next several weeks at some of the Greek words for love. Greek is a very beautiful language. It is so expressive. Many have referred to it as the perfect language. It leaves very little to the imagination because it is so precise.

As we study love, we see the precision of the Greek language in the Scriptures. As Americans, we say we love everything from our pizza to our house, and from our vehicles to our spouse. Love is used so widely that it loses some of its impact.

Even in the Scriptures, the English word, "love" appears for all the Greek words. John 21:15-17 uses two distinct and separate words in the Greek for love, yet most of our translations just say, "love." When you know the difference, the conversation takes on a whole new meaning.

We will look at three of the Greek words for love: Phileo, Agape, and Eros, and how they fit into our marriage relationship. They each have distinct meanings that should be an integral part of our marriage.

It is a very special thing for both of us to work together on this book project. We are so thankful to our Heavenly Father for teaching us these principles over the

INTRODUCTION

years. Some of them came from instruction we received in churches and at conferences, while others have come from trial and error as we continue to build our marriage as a real, personal relationship.

We do not pretend to be perfect, but we will shout from the mountain top that there is much more to experience in marriage than most are actually living on a daily basis. This is a large reason why we decided to take on this project. We have actually had people ask us about our happiness and comment that it is not natural. Well, of course, we disagree. We believe that marriage can be such a great blessing when you focus on loving the other person rather than receiving from them. Meeting their needs, instead of demanding your needs be met, your way.

Enjoy this devotional. Please let us know how God uses this to increase your love for one another and deepen the intimacy of your marriage.

Lonnie & Kim Riley

HOW TO USE THIS DEVOTIONAL

First, understand that this is a devotional for a married couple. If you are a single person, you may learn a little as you seek God for the right mate, but the intention of our heart in writing this book, is to strengthen marriages. You and your spouse should go through this material together with an open mind.

Realize that the foundation of what we teach is based on Scripture. We believe that God, the Creator of marriage, is the best source to help us understand how to love one another better in our marriages.

You will both participate in the reading every day. Take turns reading the Scripture and the lesson. We want you to read your section out loud. Let your mate hear your voice as you read. Sometimes we are using the same verse from another translation, pay attention to the subtle differences. You both enjoy hearing the other's voice, so use that to your advantage as you understand that both of you are dedicated to strengthening the love you have for each other.

The "Together Project" helps you to develop your study skills, communication, and have a common understanding. We have often found that marriages today tend to fail because husbands and wives do not adequately communicate with each other. They used to spend hours talking about their dreams, hurts, goals or whatever, then after the marriage, kids (if you have them) and careers, they begin to stop sharing. Many times marital difficulties can be ironed out if both parties will just open up and communicate. That is part of the reason for this section.

Finally, each of you prays out loud. NOT just one. Again, there is something that happens in the heart when you hear your spouse lifting you or your marriage to God in prayer. Please don't skip or skimp on this section. It may take a little time to overcome some embarrassment or timidity, but believe us it will be worth it. In order to help you get through this part, there are related prayer thoughts at the end of the lesson. These are to help "kick-start" your prayer time.

There are six lessons in each section which are intended to be completed Monday through Saturday. We feel you should pick a definite time each day when you can focus on each other. Don't try to rush through it while you are getting ready for work. Make the time to seriously go through each lesson, each day. There is nothing for you to do on Sunday. We encourage you to worship together and reflect on what God is teaching you about love and your marriage.

Our prayer is that this study will not only increase your understanding of love, but also your experience. By the end of this devotional, you should have overcome any reluctance in communication, have a greater appreciation for one another, and your intimacy level should be at its peak. Don't be shy about what God does for your marriage. Tell others how He has helped you and get several copies of this devotional and give them as gifts to those you care about.

Let us pray for you now, before you begin this process together:

"Father in heaven, we thank You for the gift of love and for the wonderful relationship of marriage, which You designed to complete us. We ask that You will prepare the hearts of the couple about to embark on this journey. May they be open, honest, sincere and obedient to what You want to do in their lives and marriage. We ask these things in the name of Jesus.
AMEN."

A true friend freely gives, advises justly, assists readily, adventures boldly, takes all patiently, defends courageously, and continues a friend unchangeably.

William Penn

Section 1

PHILEO

φιλέω
philĕō, fil-eh'-o;
To be a friend

What Makes a Friend?

"Friends love through all kinds of weather,
and families stick together in all kinds of trouble."
Proverbs 17:17 (MSG)

"A friend loves at all times,
and a brother is born for a time of adversity."
Proverbs 17:17 (NIV)

"The righteous should choose his friends carefully,
For the way of the wicked leads them astray."
Proverbs 12:26 (NKJV)

"The righteous choose their friends carefully,
but the way of the wicked leads them astray."
Proverbs 12:26 (NIV)

"Make no friendship with an angry man,
And with a furious man do not go,"
Proverbs 22:24 (NKJV)

"Don't make friends with people who have hot,
violent tempers."
Proverbs 22:24 (GNT)

This first word translated as love is the word *Phileo*, which means to be a friend. King Solomon, considered by many as the wisest man to ever live, gives a strong characteristic of friendship. Love. Not just any love, but unfailing love. Love at all times.

The first Scripture above says that real friends love us *through* all kinds of weather. They are someone who is your friend always, during both the good times and the tough ones as well. They are by your side and help you THROUGH the tough times. How they help may be by offering support, giving a truthful assessment of our situation and urge us to make necessary changes, or by just being there and helping us keep a positive attitude.

What are some of the other characteristics of someone you might consider to be a real friend? Over the years, as we have ministered to others, some of the characteristics that are continually mentioned are:

Supportive	Honest
Trustworthy	Accepting
Challenging	Respectful

How many people do you know who are friends to that degree? If asked, would any of your friends describe you as someone that has those characteristics?

TOGETHER PROJECT

Using the list given on the previous page as a starting point, write down all the additional characteristics of a true friend that the two of you can come up with.

_____

_____

_____

_____

_____

_____

_____

Make notes and discuss why these traits are important to you when desiring to build a real friendship.

_____

_____

_____

_____

_____

_____

_____

PRAY TOGETHER

1. Pray for your friends.

2. Pray for God to help you be a better friend.

3. Pray for God to send you new real friends.

The Strength of a Friend

"Two are better than one,
Because they have a good reward for their labor.
For if they fall, one will lift up his companion.
But woe to him who is alone when he falls,
For he has no one to help him up.
Again, if two lie down together, they will keep warm;
But how can one be warm alone?
Though one may be overpowered by another, two can
withstand him.
And a threefold cord is not quickly broken."
Ecclesiastes 4:9-12 (NKJV)

"It's better to have a partner than go it alone.
Share the work, share the wealth.
And if one falls down, the other helps,
But if there's no one to help, tough!
Two in a bed warm each other.
Alone, you shiver all night.
By yourself you're unprotected.
With a friend you can face the worst.
Can you round up a third?
A three-stranded rope isn't easily snapped."
Ecclesiastes 4:9-12 (MSG)

As you realized yesterday, true friends are rare. They are so rare that perhaps they should be placed on the national endangered species list along with the Relict Leopard Frog and the Copperbelly Water Snake. In this passage a true friend is likened to a reward. Have either of you ever received a reward? How did you feel? If you have not received a reward, how do you think you would feel?

Life is definitely more rewarding when you can share it with a true friend. A real friend, we are also told, is there to lift you up if you fall and to stand beside you when you go through life's battles.

Regretfully, both falling and fighting are events that are going to happen to each of us sooner or later. Perhaps we fail and others are more than willing to share the "shovel" and cover us with distasteful words and actions. This is where true friends encourage and help each other.

The New King James Version of the Scripture text uses the word "labor." Real friendship does require work, it doesn't just happen, but it will certainly be worth it in the end. Or put another way, it (friendship) will only occur when effort and purpose are invested and applied, however the dividends are significant in the long run.

TOGETHER PROJECT

Write down and discuss what kind of work or labor each of you feels is involved in developing a true friendship.

_____
_____
_____
_____
_____

Describe a time when a friend helped to lift you up. Write the name of that friend here.

_____
_____

List times when you were the kind of friend that lifts another up. (Be specific)

_____
_____
_____
_____

PRAY TOGETHER

1. Thank God for any friends that have lifted you up.

2. Pray for those friends' lives in the following ways:

   a. Their family
   b. Their health
   c. Their prosperity

3. Ask God to give both of you an opportunity to lift up a friend in need. To BE the kind of friend you would like to HAVE!

Your Real Friends

"These things I have spoken to you, that My joy may remain in you, and that your joy may be full. This is My commandment, that you love one another as I have loved you. Greater love has no one than this, than to lay down one's life for his friends. You are My friends if you do whatever I command you. No longer do I call you servants, for a servant does not know what his master is doing; but I have called you friends, for all things that I heard from My Father I have made known to you. "
John 15:11-15 (NKJV)

"I've told you these things for a purpose: that my joy might be your joy, and your joy wholly mature. This is my command: Love one another the way I loved you. This is the very best way to love. Put your life on the line for your friends. You are my friends when you do the things I command you. I'm no longer calling you servants because servants don't understand what their master is thinking and planning. No, I've named you friends because I've let you in on everything I've heard from the Father."
John 15:11-15 (MSG)

How do you think it made Peter, James or John feel when Jesus, our Lord, our Savior named all of those that were with Him as friends? Not just as "followers", "disciples" or even "Apostles", but His actual friends.

This is not just focused on this group, but to all who meet His criteria. Friendships are important in life. They help bring true fulfillment to our existence and purpose to our calling.

When you own your own business as Kim and I have done in the past, keeping a good set of books is invaluable. When you decide to apply for a loan the lending institution will most likely want a balance sheet from you. In a financial balance sheet, there is a column for assets. These are things of value that are yours and that supposedly add value to your net worth. Such things as a house, car, furniture, stocks, retirement and cash are a few assets many people have.

In life, true friends should be considered as assets. They bring value (and balance) to your life. They are rare and should be treated with respect, honor and care. They are hard to come by and you have invested so much in the relationship up to this point in your life. We are all the richer for the addition of meaningful friendships to our lives.

TOGETHER PROJECT

Take the time to do a "friend inventory" and see if each of you make a list of 5 true friends in your life.

Husband   Wife

_____   _____

_____   _____

_____   _____

_____   _____

_____   _____

Next, make a list of true friends that relate to you as a couple.

_____

_____

_____

_____

Now discuss people who you think would list you as their true friend.

_____

_____

_____

_____

PRAY TOGETHER

1. Thank God for each person on your personal list of true friends.

2. Pray for each person on your list of people as a friend to you as a couple.

3. Ask God to open up one new friendship for each of you individually and one more for you as a couple.

Jesus, a Friend

"I have loved you just as the Father has loved me. You must go on living in my love. If you keep my commandments you will live in my love just as I have kept my Father's commandments and live in his love. I have told you this so that you can share my joy, and that your happiness may be complete. This is my commandment: that you love each other as I have loved you. There is no greater love than this—that a man should lay down his life for his friends. You are my friends if you do what I tell you to do. I shall not call you servants any longer, for a servant does not share his master's confidence. No, I call you friends, now, because I have told you everything that I have heard from the Father."
John 15:11-15 (Phillips)

"One who has unreliable friends soon comes to ruin, but there is a friend who sticks closer than a brother."
Proverbs 18:24 (NIV)

"Someone with many so-called friends may end up friendless, but a true friend is closer than a brother."
Proverbs 18:24 (VOICE)

Wow! That was an amazing statement made in the Scripture in John.

Jesus calls us a friend.

Just imagine Him sitting down to make a list like you did yesterday. Think of all the possible names He could put down. From Adam and Eve, to the Apostles Paul or Timothy. I think it would be an honor to be on that list. Well, then you should feel honored because, <u>you are on His list</u>!!

He didn't have to think about it, He didn't have to weigh it out in His mind. He was sure! He knew to add you. Jesus considers your relationship very important and He wants you to realize how He views the connection you have together.

Jesus Christ, the Word made flesh, the Son of God, the Savior of the world, the King of kings and Lord of lords has called you His friend! Hold your head up and your shoulders back.

YOU ARE A FRIEND OF GOD!

TOGETHER PROJECT

List some famous or powerful people with whom you would like to be friends.

_____

_____

_____

Why did you list each one of these people?

_____

_____

_____

Discuss what it means to have Jesus as your friend.

_____

_____

_____

Was Jesus on your list yesterday? _____

What is your part of your friendship with Jesus?

_____

_____

PRAY TOGETHER

1. Thank God for Jesus as a friend.

2. Ask God to reveal to you specific ways that you can become a better friend to Jesus.

3. Praise God for the fact that your spouse is also considered one of Jesus' friends.

False Friends

"Wealth attracts friends as honey draws flies,
but poor people are avoided like a plague.
Perjury won't go unpunished.
Would you let a liar go free?
Lots of people flock around a generous person;
everyone's a friend to the philanthropist.
When you're down on your luck,
even your family avoids you—
yes, even your best friends wish you'd get lost.
If they see you coming, they look the other way—
out of sight, out of mind."
Proverbs 19:4-7 (MSG)

"All who hate me whisper together against me;
against me they devise my hurt, saying,
"A wicked thing is poured out upon him,
that when he lies down, he will not rise up again."
Even my close friend in whom I trusted,
who ate my bread,
has lifted up his heel against me."
Psalm 41:7-9 (NASB)

People will align themselves as your friends for many reasons. Some for money or power. Others for influence or a possible promotion. Some just for your attention.

Each and every one of us have had false friends at one time or another, and we have probably been a false friend as well. We have known or have become the type of person who fail the true test of friendship. This can cause great hurt and even bitterness.

In order to have freedom from the chains of emotional pain and bitterness, we must forgive those who hurt us—even if they don't ask. We forgive so that our Father in heaven will forgive us.

The bottom line is that you cannot judge another. They may seem to you to be a terrible friend. But stop and think that it could be possible that you may seem the same to them. Ouch! I know.

We are called to love, forgive and show the love and forgiveness of God. Take the time to look up and read the poem by Mother Teresa, "Do It Anyway" and make it your motto as a couple.

Remember, the very ones that Jesus came to save, were the ones who asked that He be crucified. He was betrayed by Judas Iscariot, one of the twelve. He knew the pain of false friends, yet He also prayed that the Father would forgive them because they didn't know what they were doing.

TOGETHER PROJECT

List people that have proven to be false friends in your life. Include them whether it was individually or as a couple. Beside their name, write how they failed you.

Name   How Failed You

_____

_____

_____

_____

_____

_____

Discuss how you felt at the betrayal, and your feelings now.

Talk about how Jesus must have felt because of His betrayal, and ask how you can emulate that as a couple.

PRAY TOGETHER

1. Pray for each person on the list and ask God to bless them.

2. Pray that you may forgive them

3. Ask God to show you how that friendship might be renewed.

A Mate's Best Friend

"That they admonish the young women to love their
husbands, to love their children,"
Titus 2:4 (NKJV)

"...so they may encourage the young women to love their
husbands and to love their children,"
Titus 2:4 (HCSB)

"His mouth is sweetness.
He is absolutely desirable.
This is my love,
and this is my friend,
young women of Jerusalem."
Song of Solomon 5:16 (HCSB)

"His mouth is altogether sweet,
lovable in every way.
Such, O women of Jerusalem,
is my beloved, my friend."
Song of Solomon (TLB)

As each of us were growing up we had our "best friends," known in today's culture as BFF's. This was a very fluid arrangement. It could change any moment depending on the circumstances. As we matured we had real best friends.

As we began to date/court, we hopefully developed a friendship with our dates before we were romantically "smitten." Even society has seen this importance in the past by defining our dating relationship as, "Girl friend" or "Boy friend."

In the first passage of Scripture, the older women are instructed to help wives understand that they are to love their husbands. What is unique is that the Greek word used here is phileo, to be a friend. It is important that this part of the marriage relationship be purposefully developed. We believe this applies to both sides of the relationship.

In the Song of Solomon, the bride is longing for her husband. As she expresses her desire, she makes sure that the daughters of Jerusalem also realize that she considers her husband her friend.

Man and woman should develop the concept that life-long mates should become the best of friends. Your spouse should be your BFF (best friend forever.)

TOGETHER PROJECT

Review your list of the qualities of a friend from the first lesson in this section. Discuss both if, and how, they are applicable to your marriage.

Ask your mate if they really feel like they are your best friend. If the answer is truthfully, "No," then lovingly explain why you feel that way.

Ask your mate for two (2) specific suggestions on how you can be a better friend to them. It is important that you are honest with your spouse. Do not say what you think they want to hear and keep the focus on being a better friend (not just mate, spouse or lover).

_____

_____

_____

_____

PRAY TOGETHER

1. Pray for your spouse out loud in their presence. Ask how they would appreciate being prayed for.

2. Pray that you would be the best friend your spouse has ever had.

3. Audibly thank God for the gift of your spouse. Take the time to list the great qualities of your spouse that you wish to thank God for specifically.

> *"Lord, grant that I might not so much seek to be loved as to love."*
>
> *Francis of Assisi*

Section 2

AGAPE

ἀγάπη
agape, ag-ah'-pay;
To love

Who's First?

"Therefore if you have any encouragement from being united with Christ, if any comfort from His love, if any common sharing in the Spirit, if any tenderness and compassion, then make my joy complete by being like-minded, having the same love, being one in spirit and of one mind. Do nothing out of selfish ambition or vain conceit. Rather, in humility value others above yourselves, not looking to your own interests but each of you to the interests of the others."
Philippians 2:1-4 (NIV)

"If you've gotten anything at all out of following Christ, if His love has made any difference in your life, if being in a community of the Spirit means anything to you, if you have a heart, if you care— then do me a favor: Agree with each other, love each other, be deep-spirited friends. Don't push your way to the front; don't sweet-talk your way to the top. Put yourself aside, and help others get ahead. Don't be obsessed with getting your own advantage. Forget yourselves long enough to lend a helping hand."
Philippians 2:1-4 (MSG)

The Bible tells us to regard other people over ourselves. This is even more accentuated in marriage. A woman is told to voluntarily submit herself by making her husband first in her life like she does God. This doesn't mean to be a doormat, but rather to place your husband as the head of your home, just as God is (or should be) the head of your life.

A man is told to love (Agape) his wife just like Jesus cared more about the world than His own life. He didn't give any conditions to show His love for us by dying on the cross. He made the choice to place us before Himself.

To love unconditionally means that no matter what the other person does or does not do, you choose to love them. Even if you feel they aren't putting you first, or fulfilling what the Bible says. The moment we begin to say, "They aren't putting me first," we have become selfish and placed ourselves above them. Then we have definitely placed "conditions" on our love or at least on our expression of our love to our mate.

Communication is always necessary, but unconditional love is an act of the will. A decision to put the other person before ourselves. Even when the conditions are not what we like or want. As you begin to put this type of Agape love into action God will strengthen and bless your marriage.

TOGETHER PROJECT

List ways you feel your spouse places you before themselves.

Husband   Wife

_____   _____

_____   _____

_____   _____

_____   _____

_____   _____

Discuss and list ways you can show your decision to esteem your spouse better than yourself.

_____

_____

_____

_____

_____

Who do the two of you know that has exemplified this type of self-less, unconditional love in God in their marriage?

PRAY TOGETHER

1. Pray that God would cultivate in you and your spouse the kind of love that considers the other more important.

2. Ask God to reveal to you specific ways that you can show this type of self-sacrificing love to your spouse.

3. Ask God to show each of you where you have been selfish in demanding love instead of openly giving and showing love.

4. Pray for the couple you mentioned above that has shown this kind of love in their marriage and ask God to bless them and give the two of you the courage to thank them for living this in front of you.

Patient and Kind

" Love is patient, love is kind.
It does not envy, it does not boast, it is not proud"
1 Corinthians 13:4 (NIV)

"Love is patient, love is kind and is not jealous; love does
not brag and is not arrogant"
1 Corinthians 13:4 (NASB)

" We remain pure. We understand completely what it
means to serve God. We are patient and kind. We serve
him in the power of the Holy Spirit. We serve him with
true love."
2 Corinthians 6:6 (NIRV)

"You are God's chosen people. You are holy and dearly
loved. So put on tender mercy and kindness as if they
were your clothes. Don't be proud. Be gentle and patient."
Colossians 3:12 (NIRV)

"But the kindness and love of God our Savior appeared."
Titus 3:4 (NIRV)

We have often heard, "Patience is a virtue." Yet with our mates, we seldom show this virtue. The more we know about a person and their faults and tendencies, the less patient we become. Perhaps it is because we see the person daily, we expect them to change and grow according to our schedule of thought.

Kindness is another attribute listed in today's verse. A different axiom we've heard in our lives is, "familiarity breeds contempt." The intimacy created by marriage can chip away at our kindness toward one another.

If we are honest, we may see that we are extremely more patient and allot more kind with people we don't even know. Are you able to exhibit patience with a clerk at the store more easily than with your spouse at home? Maybe it's those we work with. Are we more kind with them than we are with our spouse?

Consider how you are able to answer the telephone cheerfully and with anticipation, even when you are in the middle of an argument or dispute with your spouse. You can choose to stop your anger in order to "hide" the argument from those on the phone. If you can control it when you answer the phone, you can do it just because you choose to honor and respect your mate. We must learn to be both patient and kind with the object of our love.

TOGETHER PROJECT

List the most patient and kind people each of you know.

_____
_____
_____
_____
_____

When was the last time you were unkind and/or less than patient with each other? Tell each other when it was and how it made you feel.

_____
_____
_____
_____
_____

Are you kinder to complete strangers, a waitress, a gas station clerk, co-worker than each other? Discuss why that happens.

PRAY TOGETHER

1. Thank God for His patience and kindness towards both of you.

2. Ask God for help to be more patient with each other.

3. Pray for opportunities to show kindness toward one another.

4. Thank God for your patient and kind spouse. (In faith)

Generous and Humble

"Love is patient, love is kind and is not jealous; love does not brag and is not arrogant"
1 Corinthians 13:4 (NASB)

" Love is patient, love is kind.
It does not envy, it does not boast, it is not proud"
1 Corinthians 13:4 (NIV)

"Summing up: Be agreeable, be sympathetic, be loving, be compassionate, be humble. That goes for all of you, no exceptions. No retaliation. No sharp-tongued sarcasm. Instead, bless—that's your job, to bless. You'll be a blessing and also get a blessing.
Whoever wants to embrace life
and see the day fill up with good,
Here's what you do:
Say nothing evil or hurtful;
Snub evil and cultivate good;
run after peace for all you're worth.
God looks on all this with approval,
listening and responding well to what He's asked;
But He turns his back
on those who do evil things."
1 Peter 3:8-12 (MSG)

Humility and generosity are two more characteristics of Godly love. As a couple, we don't often think of these traits as important to our marriage. Yet, as we strive for a more intimate relationship, we must guard against envy and pride.

If we truly consider each other as more important, then we will be willing to open our hearts with generosity and to humble ourselves for the needs and wants of the other.

It doesn't take any training for a little child to cry out "mine" when another child picks up his favorite toy. We also witness teenagers continually praise themselves, and lift up their accomplishments and good deeds. Yet, maturity sets in and then as adults we see these traits and consider them an area that needs work.

In a marriage, we should give and not require from our spouse. This is a relationship built on love. As we give and hold the other person in esteem above us, the law of reciprocity is activated and our needs and desires are usually met as a consequence. However, true love does not keep that as a motive. The privilege to give and treat the other person well is enough for Godly love to grow.

TOGETHER PROJECT

Do you consider each other generous or stingy?

Give examples of each. _____

_____

_____

_____

_____

_____

How do you feel that your spouse considers you and your needs more important than their own? _____

_____

_____

_____

_____

_____

PRAY TOGETHER

1. Ask your heavenly Father to give each of you opportunities today to be generous to one another.

2. Pray that you will be sensitive to your spouse's needs and place them above your own.

3. Thank God that He has been generous in love and grace to you, and that Jesus humbled Himself (Phil. 2) and gave Himself for you. Ask for that same attitude.

Courteous and Unselfish

"Love is patient, love is kind.
It does not envy, it does not boast, it is not proud.
It does not dishonor others, it is not self-seeking, it is not
easily angered, it keeps no record of wrongs."
1 Corinthians 13:4-5 (NIV)

"Love endures long and is patient and kind; love never is
envious nor boils over with jealousy, is not boastful or
vainglorious, does not display itself haughtily.
⁵ It is not conceited (arrogant and inflated with pride); it
is not rude (unmannerly) and does not act unbecomingly.
Love (God's love in us) does not insist on its own rights or
its own way, for it is not self-seeking; it is not touchy or
fretful or resentful; it takes no account of the evil done to it
[it pays no attention to a suffered wrong]."
1 Corinthians 13:4-5 (AMP)

"Be humble and gentle.
Be patient with each other, making allowance for each
other's faults because of your love."
Ephesians 4:2 (TLB)

Mary-Kate and Ashley, the Olsen twins, were adorable in the sitcom "Full House." One of their signature statements was "How rude!" If even little children know what it is to be rude, so should we as adults.

Too often we find ourselves speaking or acting in ways that even a little child would consider rude. Not only that, but we become self-centered and demanding. The traits listed today are to be courteous and unselfish. We were all taught to say thank you and please and to share with our friends. Yet somehow, once we say "I do" we "don't." Maybe part of our pre-marital counseling should have included reading the "Miss Manners" column in the paper. Real, Godly love is polite, well-mannered, considerate, selfless, magnanimous, altruistic, and thoughtful in our relationship with each other on a daily basis. We treated each other that way while we were dating, didn't we? If we didn't we probably wouldn't have had that first date, and definitely would not have gone on a second one.

Let's be honest here, isn't that what you envisioned when you planned to spend your life together? Did you dream that you would become rude, self-centered and that your spouse would be so demanding and impolite? Consider this: the way you speak and act toward your spouse is eventually the way they will speak and act toward you.

TOGETHER PROJECT

How can you each be more courteous to one another?

Ask your mate for suggestions and write them here.

_____

_____

_____

_____

How has the way you treated each other when you were dating changed now that you are married?

_____

_____

_____

_____

Do you treat your spouse better when the "in-laws" are around? Hmmm.

PRAY TOGETHER

1. Ask for God to reveal to you where you are less than courteous to your spouse and confess that sin both to God and to your mate.

2. Ask God for grace and strength as you begin immediately to follow the suggestions made by your mate in the together time. Pray over each suggestion.

3. Pray with your spouse for blessings on them in an unselfish way.

Good Tempered - Pure in Thought

"Love is patient; love is kind.
Love isn't envious, doesn't boast, brag, or strut about.
There's no arrogance in love; it's never rude, crude, or
indecent—it's not self-absorbed.
Love isn't easily upset.
Love doesn't tally wrongs"
1 Corinthians 13:4-5 (The Voice)

"Love is very patient and kind, never jealous or envious,
never boastful or proud, never haughty or selfish or rude.
Love does not demand its own way.
It is not irritable or touchy.
It does not hold grudges and will
hardly even notice when others do it wrong"
1 Corinthians 13:4-5 (TLB)

"From now on, brothers and sisters,
if anything is excellent and if anything is admirable,
focus your thoughts on these things:
all that is true, all that is holy, all that is just,
all that is pure, all that is lovely,
and all that is worthy of praise."
Ephesians 4:8 (CEB)

Are you easily provoked? Do you fly off the handle without warning? Do you justify yourself by saying, "That's just me. I can't change." Well, yeah you can. The Bible actually says that all the old is passed away (as in dead) and you have become a new creation. No excuses. Let me ask you again, "Are you easily provoked?"

Maybe not, but do you provoke your mate?

Ouch! We all have to admit that at times we "push their button" on purpose. And, at times we act like we want our buttons to be pushed. In order to live in peace and not hurt the spirit of our mate, we must learn to keep our tempers under control.

When anger is allowed to vent, we say and do things that can cause harm to the delicate relationship we are trying to build. We tend to close up and lock out the other person and that is the direct opposite of intimacy. Not only does Satan like to tempt us to vent our anger toward each other, but his main battlefield is the mind. We should guard our thoughts and not let evil thoughts control what we think of our spouse.

True selfless love, doesn't keep score. We are to help and love each other, not remind each other of our faults, shortcomings or sins. We support one another in love. This is what we expect, so it is what we should give!

TOGETHER PROJECT

When was the last time you were really "ticked off" at your mate?

What are some real ways you can control your temper with your spouse? _____
_____
_____
_____
_____

How can you keep from "pushing" your spouse's buttons?
_____
_____
_____
_____

How has Satan tempted you to think evil of your mate or keep score? _____
_____

PRAY TOGETHER

1. Ask God for forgiveness for being ill-tempered toward your mate. (Now ask your mate for forgiveness too.)

2. Praise God for the times you were good tempered toward your spouse.

3. Pray through Philippians 4:8 on page 60.

All, Never

"Though I speak with the tongues of men and of angels, but have not love, I have become sounding brass or a clanging cymbal. And though I have the gift of prophecy, and understand all mysteries and all knowledge, and though I have all faith, so that I could remove mountains, but have not love, I am nothing. And though I bestow all my goods to feed the poor, and though I give my body to be burned, but have not love, it profits me nothing. Love suffers long and is kind; love does not envy; love does not parade itself, is not puffed up; does not behave rudely, does not seek its own, is not provoked, thinks no evil; does not rejoice in iniquity, but rejoices in the truth; bears all things, believes all things, hopes all things, endures all things. Love never fails. But whether there are prophecies, they will fail; whether there are tongues, they will cease; whether there is knowledge, it will vanish away. For we know in part and we prophesy in part. But when that which is perfect has come, then that which is in part will be done away. When I was a child, I spoke as a child, I understood as a child, I thought as a child; but when I became a man, I put away childish things. For now we see in a mirror, dimly, but then face to face. Now I know in part, but then I shall know just as I also am known. And now abide faith, hope, love, these three; but the greatest of these is love."

1 Corinthians 13 (NKJV)

Allot can be said from this passage of Scripture. It has been read at countless weddings. It is one of the most beautiful and complete definitions of our Heavenly Father's gift of Agape love, poured out on us by His Holy Spirit.

"All" and "never" are strong words. The underlying truth is one of attitude. As we learn to love each other with a Godly, Agape love, we are encouraged to work through all things and never fail. This requires attitudes of consistency and determination.

One of the real problems that society is facing is that certain things are not worth working their way through. Some actions are considered irreparable, and we throw up our hands and quit. The number one cause cited for divorce these days seems to be "irreconcilable differences." People are too willing to just give up and stop trying.

We learn here that we should never fail and that we should work through all things. Not just some things, or when we feel like it. In order to build the intimate marriage we know God has planned for us, we must work through all challenges and never make the decision to give up on our love.

We have to ask God to give us His heart of love. His love never fails. He never gives up. He is always consistent and constantly by our side in love!

TOGETHER PROJECT

Is there anything your spouse could do that you wouldn't be willing to work through? _____

_____

_____

_____

_____

_____

Have you decided that something in your relationship is never going to change, so you just grin and bear it?

_____

_____

_____

_____

_____

How does your mate communicate to you that they really are committed to the vow, "Till death do us part"?

_____

_____

_____

_____

PRAY TOGETHER

1. Praise God for a love like His that will work through everything.

2. Pray through those things you listed as items that will never change and you must bear with them. Pray for both yourself and your spouse to be able to address those things in love.

3. Thank God for a spouse that is committed to a love that will never fail.

"You are my best friend as well as my lover, and I do not know which side of you I enjoy the most. I treasure each side, just as I have treasured our life together."

Nicholas Sparks

Section 3

EROS

ἔρως
eros, air-os;
Sexual love and desire

God's Plan

*"Then God saw everything that He had made, and indeed
it was very good. So the evening and the morning were
the sixth day."*
*And the LORD God said, 'It is not good that man should
be alone; I will make him a helper comparable to him.
Therefore a man shall leave his father and mother and
be joined to his wife, and they shall become one flesh.'
And they were both naked, the man and his wife, and
were not ashamed."*
Genesis 1:31; 2:18, 24, 25 (NKJV)

*"And the man and his wife were both naked and were not
embarrassed or ashamed in each other's presence."*
Genesis 2:25 (AMP)

*"The Man said,
"Finally! Bone of my bone,
flesh of my flesh!
Name her Woman
for she was made from Man."
Therefore a man leaves his father and mother and
embraces his wife. They become one flesh.
The two of them, the Man and his Wife, were naked, but
they felt no shame."*
Genesis 2:23-25 (MSG)

Understand from the very beginning of this week as we study "Eros" that sex is not bad. God created it and called it very good. You no doubt recognize the similarity of the Greek word "Eros" to the English word "Erotic".

Always remember that sex is not the most important part of marriage. It cannot create instant intimacy. Sex will not adequately resolve your fights. It definitely is not a replacement for intimate communication. It can, however, enhance all of these.

Fulfilling love-making can bring all of those areas to a higher, more satisfying level. Great sex does not ensure a great marriage, but a great marital companionship and a right relationship with God can provide the foundation for fantastic love-making!

Although sex is a wonderful part of God's plan for your marriage, it should not be demanded or "used" as a way to feel love from your spouse. The misuse of sex is bad like the misuse of money, emotions, food... the list can go on and on. Keep this in mind as we work through this topic all week. Everything taught and discussed about "Eros" is to be considered with the other two types of love in mind. Great friends dedicated to a self-less, unconditional, Godly love will create the right atmosphere for these discussions.

TOGETHER PROJECT

Does the word "sex" make you uncomfortable? Why or why not? _____

_____

_____

_____

_____

How were each of you taught about sex?

_____

_____

_____

_____

_____

Can the two of you comfortably discuss your sex life?

_____

_____

Discuss this statement, "God loved us so much that He created sex for our enjoyment."

PRAY TOGETHER

1. Ask God for an open mind about sex.

2. Ask God to reveal where YOU need to change (not your spouse).

3. Pray for a loving and giving relationship that can be expressed through wonderful, fulfilling sex.

Trust

Adam: At last, a suitable companion, a perfect partner.
Bone from my bones.
Flesh from my flesh.
I will call this one "woman" as an eternal reminder
that she was taken out of man.
Now this is the reason a man leaves his father and his
mother, and is united with his wife; and the two become
one flesh.
In those days the man and his wife were both naked and
were not ashamed.
Genesis 2:23-25 (VOICE)

The man said,
"Her bones have come from my bones.
Her body has come from my body.
She will be named 'woman,'
because she was taken out of a man."
24 That's why a man will leave his father and mother and
be joined to his wife. The two of them will become one.
25 The man and his wife were both naked. They didn't feel
any shame.
Genesis 2:23-25 (NIRV)

God made both of you and designed you to complete each other. There must be a lot of trust in any deep relationship, even more so in marriage where we leave the parents we've trusted in all our lives for a new partner.

In sexuality, that trust rises to a new level never experienced before. To be "naked and not ashamed" before our spouse is the expression of great trust. We trust them to value our feelings, accept our bodies, to touch us lovingly, to protect us from pain and to be the partner in love-making that will allow us to express ourselves openly and experience the heights of sexual gratification.

We must guard that trust. Things we say or do throughout the day or week can erode that fragile confidence. If we cannot be trusted in other, less delicate matters of life and marriage, we undermine our partner's conviction that we are trustworthy in bed.

This level of trust also requires that we keep our sexual intimacy private in our marriage. It is NOT a topic of conversation with anyone except your mate. We must guard the trust we have from our spouse well. If that is violated, it will take time before there is healing in our relationship and trust is rebuilt.

TOGETHER PROJECT

Each of you answer the following questions honestly and openly. Have either of you violated the other's trust by:

Making unkind remarks about their body?

Abusing your privilege of touching their bodies?

Causing physical pain to get your own needs met?

Expecting certain expression from the other?

Demanding certain sexual acts the other didn't feel like giving?

Being unconcerned about the fulfillment of the other?

If so, discuss this, understand their feelings.

Ask for forgiveness for violating their trust.

Ask for a new and open communication in regard to sex.

PRAY TOGETHER

1. Repent to God for any and all violations of trust discussed.

2. Thank God for the trust of your spouse, and ask Him to make you more sensitive to their needs.

3. Pray that God would help your sex life get better.

Pure-Sex

"Finally, brothers and sisters, fill your minds with beauty and truth. Meditate on whatever is honorable, whatever is right, whatever is pure, whatever is lovely, whatever is good, whatever is virtuous and praiseworthy."
Philippians 4:8 (The Voice)

"Finally, my brothers and sisters, always think about what is true. Think about what is noble, right and pure. Think about what is lovely and worthy of respect. If anything is excellent or worthy of praise, think about those kinds of things."
Philippians 4:8 (NIRV)

"Summing it all up, friends, I'd say you'll do best by filling your minds and meditating on things true, noble, reputable, authentic, compelling, gracious—the best, not the worst; the beautiful, not the ugly; things to praise, not things to curse. Put into practice what you learned from Me, what you heard and saw and realized. Do that, and God, who makes everything work together, will work you into His most excellent harmonies."
Philippians 4:8-9 (MSG)

Purity is not a word often associated with sex, but it can be. Especially in the realm of your motives. If you indeed love your spouse, that love, not your physical needs, should drive your love-making. The other person becomes the first priority. Sounds like Agape doesn't it? Meeting their needs in a way that brings them the most pleasure is the objective.

Purity can also relate to our thoughts <u>during</u> love-making. Our thoughts should center on both our partner's needs and our feelings, but they should never stray to others, pictures we have seen, or movies we have watched. Sexual overtones can be found in everything from television commercials to social media. We are bombarded by society's standards of what is desirable, beautiful and sexy. Guard your mind and intimacy well! Never pollute it with the uncleanness of the world.

"The weapons I fight with are not the weapons the world uses. In fact, it is just the opposite. My weapons have the power of God to destroy the camps of the enemy. I destroy every claim and every reason that keeps people from knowing God. I keep every thought under control in order to make it obey Christ."
2 Corinthians 10:4-5 (NIRV)

Often, as you focus to meet your mate's needs you will find a new exhilaration and satisfaction in what you feel and receive.

TOGETHER TIME

Talk to your mate about any impure thoughts you have had during sexual relations. Be understanding and supportive of one another as you step out in trust and honesty.

Discuss how you can avoid those thoughts in the future.

Discover each other's real needs and wants during sex, so that you may focus on those.

Promise to be accountable to your spouse and tell them when you have allowed your mind to wonder. Keep the focus on helping each other, not blaming each other.

PRAY TOGETHER

1. Ask God to guard your mind during sex.

2. Pray for your spouse's weaknesses in this area. Cover their mind in loving prayer. Pray through 2 Corinthians 10:4-5 quoted on page 79.

3. Ask God for an attitude of acceptance and understanding between each other as you battle the power of the mind together.

Best Sex

"Marriage is honorable among all,
and the bed undefiled;"
Hebrews 13:4a (NKJV)

"Marriage is honorable in every respect;
and, in particular, sex within marriage is pure."
Hebrews 13:4a (CJB)

"Marriage is to be honored by all,
and husbands and wives must be faithful to each other."
Hebrews 13:4 (GNT)

"Marriage is honorable in every way,
so husbands and wives should be faithful to each other"
Hebrews 13:4 (NOG)

Humans have strong memories. Sometimes we let hurtful memories cloud out any good ones. On the contrary, others have been known to so concentrate on the good as to have no recollection of any bad times. Too often in the realm of sex, we have a tendency to focus on past negative experiences of love-making with our spouse. Hurtful, clumsy, messy times.

It will encourage us to periodically think and talk about our positive experiences. The times when both of you were satisfied and you "felt the earth move."

We may never be able to completely re-enact those special times, but we can learn from them. By sharing the things that created that type of desire or mood, we can focus on helping our mate in those ways again. Even during those special, intimate times, we can guide one another with our words and actions.

It is our contention that once the other levels of love (both the *Phileo* and *Agape*) are applied, then the stage is set for the possibility of enhancing a couples love-making and intimacy beyond their dreams, and all in keeping with God's special plan for marriage.

TOGETHER TIME

Each of you describe in detail the best sex you've ever had with each other. Close your eyes if it helps you focus or get over any embarrassment.

Explain why it was so great and discuss how that sort of experience can be had again.

Plan a special evening together in which you focus on helping each other feel that way again.

PRAY TOGETHER

1. Thank God for your mate and your love together.

2. Specifically thank Him for those special great times of sex together.

3. Ask God to help you each be more sensitive, spontaneous and open to experience even greater love-making.

That's The Way I Like It

"but, speaking the truth in love,"
Ephesians 4:15a (NKJV)

"And you shall know the truth, and the truth shall make you free."
John 8:32 (NKJV)

"Instead, we will speak the truth in love."
Ephesians 4:15a (NIRV)

Rather, let our lives lovingly express truth [in all things, speaking truly, dealing truly, living truly].
Enfolded in love, let us grow up in every way and in all things into Him Who is the Head, [even] Christ (the Messiah, the Anointed One).
Ephesians 4:15 (AMP)

Just one visit to a restaurant will open your eyes to people's various preferences. Some are:

Coffee:	regular or decaf
	black or cream
	sugar or plain
Tea:	sweet or un-sweet
	regular or decaf
	lemon or not
Steak:	well done, medium well,
	medium, medium rare, rare
Other food:	fried, broiled, boiled,
	steamed, raw, chilled

We all like different things in different ways and sometimes it depends on the occasion or our mood. It would be ridiculous to assume our waiter knew exactly what we wanted and how. We must communicate to him, and even then it's not always right. He is human you know!

Oh, how much more is communication necessary in the realm of sex. Often we are "served" what we don't want, don't like or do want some other way, because we don't communicate. We expect our spouse to be the super lover who knows and sees all. Not so! Communication is important at every level of the marriage—including sex.

TOGETHER PROJECT

Discuss your sexual likes and dislikes in an open and understanding way.

Create your own method of communication during sex. (whisper, touch, movement, etc.)

How does it make you feel when your spouse has a suggestion on what they would like better?

Are the two of you becoming more comfortable talking and expressing yourself in relation to your sex life?

PRAY TOGETHER

1. Thank God for communication and the fact that it builds oneness and trust.

2. Ask God to make you the lover your spouse needs.

3. Ask God to guard you against rejection when suggestions are made.

4. Pray for your spouse to trust you and be open with you when you are intimate.

What is Sexy?

"Your spring water is for you and you only,
not to be passed around among strangers.
Bless your fresh-flowing fountain!
Enjoy the wife you married as a young man!
Lovely as an angel, beautiful as a rose—
don't ever quit taking delight in her body.
Never take her love for granted!"
Proverbs 5:17-19 (MSG)

"Yes, and yours are, too—my love's kisses
flow from his lips to mine.
I am my lover's.
I'm all he wants. I'm all the world to him!
Come, dear lover—
let's tramp through the countryside.
Let's sleep at some wayside inn,
then rise early and listen to bird-song.
Let's look for wildflowers in bloom,
blackberry bushes blossoming white,
Fruit trees festooned
with cascading flowers.
And there I'll give myself to you,
my love to your love!"
Song of Solomon 7:9-12 (MSG)

If you asked 100 people the question, "What is sexy?", you'd probably get 100 different answers. To some it's attitude, others may say clothes or perfume/cologne. Still some think it's a car or candlelight, or maybe some even think it's lingerie or spontaneity.

Even a cursory glance at the supermarket will reveal our nation's interest in what is sexy. There are titles of "Sexiest Man Alive" or "Sexiest Woman Alive" where the people are voted on by the readers of the magazine. It is safe to say that our culture has taken this question to an unhealthy level.

But, really it isn't important what 100 or even 10 million others think. You have only one partner in life, love, marriage and sex. You need to know what they regard as sexy. Don't do for them what you think is sexy, find out what they think is sexy and what isn't. This helps your mate be more attracted toward you and increases their desire and participation during sexual relations.

Once again, this requires the trust. It may even be the ultimate trust of being able to communicate about things that can be embarrassing or difficult. "*Agape*" love is needed here.

TOGETHER PROJECT

What are some of the things you think your spouse regards as sexy?

Candidly share and list exactly what you find sexy and is helpful in putting you in the mood for sex.

Openly discuss what is not sexy to you that your partner has done.

PRAY TOGETHER

1. Thank God for your spouse's sexuality.

2. Thank Him for open communication and ask Him to guard your spirits as you become vulnerable before one another.

3. Thank God for creating sex.

> *"Accustom yourself continually to make many acts of love, for they enkindle and melt the soul."*
>
> *Saint Teresa of Avila*

Section 4

ACTION

Love in Action, is a Verb.

Water the seed and watch it grow.

"Just Because I Love You" Card

I first heard of this exercise on a retreat for youth leaders. It brings a little fun and creativity into the relationship, and shows love in a tangible way. Once a couple understands their love as the Father has designed it, it is only natural that they desire the best for each other and to serve one another.

One unique way of showing this to one another is the "Just Because I Love You" card. This is how it is to be used. As a marriage progresses, we all seem to take on responsibilities, little chores that become our "job." As a result of that, our mate usually leaves that item undone around the house because it's not their job."

Maybe she does the laundry and he takes out the garbage. Perhaps he feeds or washes the dog and she cleans the house. I've known some couples that decide: He takes care of the outside and she takes care of the inside. Whatever the situation, in order to make this work, you must realize what each other's jobs are.

Next, there should only be one card for the couple to use, <u>not two</u>. Let the husband start with the card. He decides to do one of "her jobs" for the wife without her knowing it or seeing him do it. He then leaves the card in a conspicuous place so that she knows what he has done. Then the card now belongs to her.

The wife now looks for opportunities to show her love for him by doing his work. The cycle continues. At times it may be a little gift, or something the person needs. The focus is to show love in a tangible way, not just on special occasions.

Once you get the hang of it, it will be fun. You will begin to think different ways to show your love. You will also love being surprised when you go to do your "chore" and find that it is already done and the card let's you know why.

This love "action" is one that can be easily used along with one of the other actions. We will show you a couple of ways as we take you through the additional actions this week.

There is a card in the appendix of this book that can be cut out and used just for this exercise, or just copied and placed on a 3 x 5 note card. You could even use the perforated business card stock you can purchase at an office store and make several of them, because once you get started in this, it can be addictive. May it be used so much, that it wears out and you have to replace it frequently.

TOGETHER TIME

Make a list of the "chores" that each of you have assumed the responsibility for doing.

Husband   Wife

_____

_____

_____

_____

_____

_____

_____

_____

PRAY TOGETHER

1. Thank God for your spouse's willingness to complete the responsibilities you listed above.

2. Ask God where you can lighten your spouse's burdens and carry more of their load.

3. Seek God in where you can show your love by doing your spouse's chores, "Just Because" you love them.

Date Night

When we first decide that we are attracted to the person we eventually marry, we spent time together. A lot of time together, mostly on dates. Just the two of us. We were oblivious to the world around us. We just focused on spending time together. For a majority of us, we were younger and had teenage jobs. We couldn't spend a lot of money (we didn't have any). But we were creative and found good ways to spend time together with the person we were falling in love with. It really didn't matter how much was spent, we were just wanting to be together.

Then life happens. The wedding planning consumes us (and our money). Then moving into a house or apartment, working our jobs, taking care of the home, doing the laundry, cooking meals, mowing the grass, etc. The relationship we took so much time to build, now takes a back-seat to the rest of our "responsibilities."

Next, most of us began our own family and the children arrived. Now we have a whole new set of responsibilities and a schedule that is not very flexible. School, sports, music or dance lessons add infinity and beyond and our lives just get busier and busier. Yet in reality, the most important investment we can make for our marriage is to continue to spend time together.

We encourage you to make special time to date your spouse. Put it on the calendar in red ink. Do not allow anything to become more important. Get a babysitter if you have to. You don't have to spend a lot of money if you are strapped. Pack a picnic. Walk through the park. Go to the "cheap" movies. Send the kids away for the evening and curl up on the couch together and watch a movie. Light some candles and put some music on. How long has it been since you just enjoyed talking, snuggling and even slow dancing?

Be creative like you were before you were married. The main focus is to spend time together. Do it once a week, or every other week. Make it special. Anticipate the time and it will be rewarding. You can even take turns planning the evening so that you don't stall over where to eat or what to do. That way you will focus on your mate and think about the things they like to do, places they like to go, and food they like to eat. You can even use the "Just Because Card" in tandem with this. If your spouse will enjoy the night out even more if they know the things they have to do once they get home are already taken care of, they can just relax and take pleasure in your company.

If you have children, you will be setting an example for their future marriage. They will understand the importance of making one another the priority. You teach by example and they never forget it.

TOGETHER TIME

Make a list of a dozen things you could do together. Be creative and consider what the other person likes to do as well.

1. _____   2. _____

3. _____   4. _____

5. _____   6. _____

7. _____   8. _____

9. _____   10. _____

11. _____   12. _____

Be sure to include a few things that don't require much money so you can continue when things are tight.

Decide on the frequency of your dates and what night works best for both of you and write it down.

_____
_____
_____

PRAY TOGETHER

1. Ask God to help you make the commitment to date your spouse.

2. Pray that God will help you prioritize dating into your schedule.

3. Thank God in advance for the benefits of dating your spouse.

Coupon Book

Our society has fallen in love with the coupon. There are people who excel at finding, clipping and maximizing the value of coupons by shopping where they double or triple the value. Both my mailbox and my newspapers are constantly overflowing with page after page of coupons. Now you can have them delivered through your email.

You can add a spark of excitement into your marriage just by making a little book of coupons. Begin by creating a list of things that you know your spouse enjoys. Make a small book and allow them to "redeem" the coupon any time they want.

It can be simple things like, "a night off from washing the dishes," "a day off from doing laundry," or "a week off from mowing the grass." It can be even more personal like, "a day at the spa," "a day of golf," or "a dinner out at the place of your choice." Perhaps it can even have sexual overtones like, "a romantic get away at the beach or mountains," "an evening of romance at home without the kids," or "a lingerie shopping trip."

Most of the coupons we receive at our home have fine print. Sometimes you have to buy two dinners and two sodas to get the offer. Other times the coupon will expire at the end of the month or season. You can have fun with this. Make your terms and conditions funny and lighthearted. There is no real expiration to your love or your desire to serve your spouse, but you can be creative and say things like, "Good until our 50th wedding anniversary" or something like that. Make it cute and make it applicable to your lives.

Find out what your spouse really appreciates and add that. Enjoy the thrill of being able to meet your spouse's needs whenever they pull out that coupon. This is a great way to help your spouse communicate what they want or need, without a long, drawn out conversation.

All they have to do is tear out the coupon and hand it to you. Spice it up! Don't just offer what you want, but think of what they would enjoy. Prove that you are willing to take the "back seat" and focus on their wants, desires and likes. Make it all about your spouse, and you will be surprised how it will also help you, as you take care of them.

Spend some time thinking about your delivery as well. You could wrap up the little booklet and leave it somewhere conspicuous with the "Just Because I Love You" card on top. You can actually send it in the mail. Men, you can even drop it by the florist and have them attach it to a bouquet of flowers. Ladies, he is sure to find it if you put it near the television remote. If you are computer savvy, you can create it and send it via email. Just put some thought into it and it will make it even more special for your love.

TOGETHER TIME

Make a list of things each of you enjoy and for which you would love to receive a coupon.

Husband	Wife
_____	_____
_____	_____
_____	_____
_____	_____
_____	_____
_____	_____
_____	_____
_____	_____
_____	_____

PRAY TOGETHER

1. Ask God to help you think unselfishly about what your spouse would enjoy. It has nothing to do with your preference.

2. Pray that God will help you fulfill your coupon promises with an attitude of love, not duty.

3. Be grateful to God for the opportunity to bless your mate and to make your spouse feel your great love for them.

Romantic Getaway

Real romance is not always sporadic nor is it necessarily random. It really takes thought, energy and planning. We have all seen a romantic candlelight dinner on a movie or television show. The table is set, flowers are in the center, and sometimes there are candles on the table and all around the room. Usually there is some type of slow, low music playing in the background. Well, none of that just shows up. Someone had to get the flowers, set the table, choose the music and light the candles. It was all the result of planning and thoughtfulness.

Make the effort to design a short getaway that is totally focused on romance. In this world of easy travel and travel agencies always competing over your dollar, you can get some great deals for just a little money.

As you think this through, consider all the factors. Where can you go that will fit into your budget? Is there a place nearby so you don't have to spend hours and hours driving? Consider the weather.

Since we live in a resort/beach town, we are very familiar with the season vs. off season rates. In Myrtle Beach an oceanfront room that would cost you $150.00 or more during the summer, can be had at half that in the fall and almost a quarter of that during the winter.

There are other factors and items to think about for a romantic trip. Think beyond just sex. This is also a time of walking together, talking with one another, and holding hands. Remember the little things that your mate may enjoy like candles, perfume/cologne, lingerie, or music.

If you have children, make sure they are cared for by someone you trust wholeheartedly. This is a biggie if the guy is planning this trip. You don't want your bride to be overly concerned about the kids. NOT romantic.

Make a plan, but be flexible with it. This is not about getting things accomplished. It's about getting closer, reducing stress, and focusing on your spouse. Try to plan just a few days, not always a full week. You can afford to do it more often if you stay close to home and keep it to a couple of days with little overhead.

If your budget will allow, consider doing this once a quarter, or at the very least every six months. Perhaps you can take turns scheduling and planning the getaways so that there is some mystery as well as shared responsibility for this time together. This will help you keep focused on the other person. Each of you will get a chance to show how important it is to understand your spouse's likes, dislikes and preferences.

Please don't EVER include friends or family on your trip. That is for another time. This is about the two of you only. Trust us, you need this time alone together.

TOGETHER TIME

Create a listing of a half dozen nearby places you both would enjoy going to on a romantic trip.

_____

_____

_____

_____

_____

_____

Make tentative plans for the first trip. Do this one together and make it happen now. Place your plans here.

_____

_____

_____

_____

_____

_____

Decide who will be responsible for planning the next one.

PRAY TOGETHER

1. Pray that God will open the financial resources to make this small trip for the good of your relationship.

2. Ask God to grant you favor as you are looking to book your trip.

3. Thank God in advance for the wonderful, intimate time you will have with your friend, lover, and soul-mate.

Retreat or Conference

There are many ministries that focus on building great marriages. They have designed retreats or conferences with that in mind. Find several of these, do some research on the topics or sessions they intend to focus on and plan to attend at least one that you are both interested in each year. It can be a cost, so plan ahead. Invest in your relationship.

God can use these times away to strengthen your relationship. He can reveal any areas of weakness or trouble that have developed and guide you in overcoming them. Then again, sometimes we just need a little help recognizing where we have allowed the things of this world and the cares of life to slip back in a place of priority that takes away from our spouse and our marriage.

Here are a few nationally known organizations that have a proven, biblical and effective ministry of supporting and fortifying your marriage:

www.familylife.com

www.moodyconferences.com

www.focusonthefamily.com

You can also do a Google search for "Christian marriage retreats" and find an event that will work for the two of you. We recently tried it and it actually yielded 18 million hits. If finances are tight, try to keep it close and off peak season. You should also keep our website in mind (www.fmintl.org) as we are seeking to develop a marriage retreat here at the beach.

Most of these conferences understand that you need some time away as well. They will usually make the schedule somewhat flexible so that you can have dinner together or have some quality time to share what is happening in your mind and heart at the conference.

Keep an open mind as you attend the conference. Ask God to work in you through the sessions. Sometimes it is in the little things that a golden nugget of information can be found to change your relationship for the better. God can use a song, a testimony or a new friendship just as much as He can use the "Keynote Speaker." Focus on what you can do to make your marriage relationship better. Don't focus on what you think your spouse needs. Get out of the conference what God intends for you to receive.

TOGETHER TIME

Make a list of ministries that offer various marriage retreats or conferences that both of you would like to attend.

_____

_____

_____

_____

_____

Make tentative plans for one of the retreats or conferences. Do this together and place your plans here.

_____

_____

_____

_____

_____

Consider speaking to your pastor and having a ministry like ours come to your church for a weekend and have a marriage seminar. The cost would be less and you would have a community of fellow believers to help each other in the growth process.

PRAY TOGETHER

1. Pray for God's guidance in choosing the right conference for your marriage.

2. Pray that God will open the financial resources to make your attendance possible to strengthen your marriage.

3. Thank God in advance for showing each of you ways to make your marriage relationship better.

4. Pray for your pastor to see the value of holding a seminar at your church.

Serve Together

Through His discourses with the Apostles, Jesus reveals that it is important to have a "servant's heart" toward each other, and to everyone. When you choose to unselfishly serve others together, you experience peace, contentment and a sense of purpose for your life.

When you begin to serve together you will also develop a deeper bond that strengthens your marriage. There's a special intimacy that comes with working together on a service project or giving together to those in need. Spouses who embrace God's call to serve others experience an added closeness, and there are special moments and memories that naturally come when you do things together.

This intimacy is found because it is self-less. On one hand you let down your guard. As you are involved in the service project, you are not quite as self-conscious as you may be in church or at a bible study. If you are painting a house or room for someone who is disabled, you will probably get paint on you and may even look a little rag tag.

You will also have the opportunity to see the same about your spouse. Even in our marriages we can build a sense of protection or walls around us. Getting out and serving begins to bring those walls down and expose the real loving person we married.

Participating in ministry opportunities – whether in your church, neighborhood, community or the world – will help you to grow in your faith as a couple. Working side-by-side to fulfill the Great Commission (in whatever capacity) will deepen your spiritual intimacy.

Serving is about setting aside time in our busy schedules to share God's love with others and meeting their needs. Start with a small project so that you don't jump in too fast and possibly overextend yourselves. This can cause negative effects on your marriage, so be smart and prayerful. It takes time, a little planning, real commitment and a bit of sacrifice, but the results of serving together deepens your relationship and causes you to communicate on levels you normally wouldn't.

Keep an open mind as you serve. Sometimes couples may find that they have a real burden for that type of project and want to do it more often or make a longer commitment. Some have even gone on short-term (one week or so) missions trips to either the inner-city or another country only to realize that God was leading them to devote their lives to that type of ministry. God is perfectly able to make you a great servant, reveal your purpose, direct your path AND develop your marriage on a deeper level all at the same time.

TOGETHER TIME

List the areas in which you already serve together.

_____
_____
_____
_____

Discuss and list ways that you can serve together in your community or church as a couple.

_____
_____
_____
_____

Discuss and list ways that you can serve together in a short term missions project.

_____
_____
_____
_____

Choose one ministry opportunity and plan together how to get started. _____

_____
_____
_____

PRAY TOGETHER

1. Thank God in advance for allowing you an opportunity to serve with your spouse.

2. Praise Him for deepening your relationship, spiritual intimacy and communication through your service to others.

3. Pray for His direction in where to serve together.

"*Marriage is not a noun; it's a verb. It isn't something you get. It's something you do. It's the way you love your partner every day.*"

Barbara De Angelis

Edify and Bless

"Words kill, words give life; they're either poison or fruit—
you choose."
Proverbs 18:21 (MSG)

We all desire to hear that we are loved, valued, and needed. The power of positive communication can set your marriage on a path of long term growth and stability. Likewise, negative communication will cause your mate emotional pain, and the flow of malicious words could destroy your marriage. By neglecting to build your spouse up verbally, you are ignoring their need for loving affirmation and genuine affection. This may require stepping outside of your comfort zone. However, the end result is rewarding. Your spouse will grow and flourish with life-giving words of praise.

Along with edifying your spouse, you should also bless them. This means to speak well of them and to respond with good words - even when the other persons' speech may be harsh, critical, or insulting. Other ways to bless your spouse are by doing nice things for them, showing your appreciation and gratitude, and praying for them.

We are called to bless our spouse regardless of how they treat us. The more we strive to treat our mate as God intended and speak "life" to them with positive words, the more He is able to bless our marriage.

WHAT'S LOVE GOT TO DO WITH IT

As a last sort of together time, we want you to think of a time when your spouse edified and/or blessed you so that you were lifted up and felt appreciated. Take the time right now to share it with one another.

Next, think about any time when your spouse has said something to you that seemed malicious or insulting? Tell each other when it was and how it made you feel. Ask for one another's forgiveness as well as God's.

Now, in order to be proactive and not just reactive, make a list of definite ways that you can edify (build up) your mate. Place a copy of your part of that list in a couple of prominent places where you will see it often. This will become a motivator for you to take the initiative to bless and edify your spouse.

As we bring these four weeks to a close, we want to thank you for allowing us to speak into your marriage. Our goal is that you have become better friends, lovers, and selfless mates.

May your union grow in quality as you continue to understand what LOVE has to do with it. As one final act of pouring into your relationship, we are going to pray for you. We believe that God directed us to write this for specific people, YOU. So we want to bless and encourage you now through prayer.

"Dear Heavenly Father: Thank You for this wonderful couple that has taken the initiative and learned how to better love one another. We ask that You continue to bless their marriage. Teach them to bless each other and to speak life-giving words to each other. May their awesome marriage be a witness to everyone they know.

In Jesus' name we pray. AMEN"

Just Because
I Love You

SCHEDULE

DR. & MRS. RILEY

FOR YOUR EVENTS

Kim and Lonnie are open for scheduling for the following events:

- ➤ Book Signings
- ➤ Speaking engagements for your group/congregation
- ➤ Concerts
- ➤ Marriage Seminars

For information on scheduling visit

www.fmintl.org

Also Available On Amazon.com

DR. LONNIE E. RILEY

THE
EXTRAORDINARY
POWER OF

1%

40 Motivational Studies
That Can Change Your Life
1% At A Time.

Also Available On Amazon.com

Yes, You Can!

You Just Need Help

A Guide to
Personal Accountability

DR. LONNIE E. RILEY

Author of *The Extraordinary Power of 1%*

COMING SOON

ABOUT THE AUTHORS

Dr. Lonnie E. Riley is the Executive Director of Freedom Ministries International. He is a prolific author, song writer and teacher. His experience as a church planter (starting or aiding in 5 congregations) gives him a unique perspective on evangelism, church growth and the methodology the Church as a whole is utilizing in these last days.

Rev. Kimberly T. Riley is the Assistant Director of Freedom Ministries International. She has a beautiful voice and has led worship in many different arenas. Her heart for worship also includes writing songs and interpretive dance.

Their family consists of 3 grown sons; Jason (wife Kymberly), Joshua, and Randall. Kim and Lonnie presently make their home in Myrtle Beach, SC.

www.ingramcontent.com/pod-product-compliance
Lightning Source LLC
LaVergne TN
LVHW021351080426
835508LV00020B/2232